Acting Edition

What to Send Up
When it Goes Down

by Aleshea Harris

D1453092

ǀǀ SAMUEL FRENCH ǀǀǀ

No one shall make any changes in this title(s) for the purpose of production. No part of this book may be reproduced, stored in a retrieval system, scanned, uploaded, or transmitted in any form, by any means, now known or yet to be invented, including mechanical, electronic, digital, photocopying, recording, videotaping, or otherwise, without the prior written permission of the publisher. No one shall share this title(s), or any part of this title(s), through any social media or file hosting websites.

For all inquiries regarding motion picture, television, online/digital and other media rights, please contact Concord Theatricals Corp.

MUSIC AND THIRD-PARTY MATERIALS USE NOTE

Licensees are solely responsible for obtaining formal written permission from copyright owners to use copyrighted music and/or other copyrighted third-party materials (e.g., artworks, logos) in the performance of this play and are strongly cautioned to do so. If no such permission is obtained by the licensee, then the licensee must use only original music and materials that the licensee owns and controls. Licensees are solely responsible and liable for clearances of all third-party copyrighted materials, including without limitation music, and shall indemnify the copyright owners of the play(s) and their licensing agent, Concord Theatricals Corp., against any costs, expenses, losses and liabilities arising from the use of such copy-righted third-party materials by licensees. For music, please contact the appropriate music licensing authority in your territory for the rights to any incidental music.

IMPORTANT BILLING AND CREDIT REQUIREMENTS

If you have obtained performance rights to this title, please refer to your licensing agreement for important billing and credit requirements.

WHAT TO SEND UP WHEN IT GOES DOWN was developed at Automata Residency Project in Los Angeles, California in November 2015 and received its world premiere at Los Angeles's Harriet Tubman Center for Social Justice on November 13, 2015. The director was Aleshea Harris. The stage manager was Anthony Dawahare.

WHAT TO SEND UP WHEN IT GOES DOWN received its New York premiere at the Movement Theatre Company (Producing Artistic Leadership Team: Eric Lockley, Deadria Harrington, David Mendizábal, Taylor Reynolds) at A.R.T./New York Theatres in New York City on November 11, 2018. The director was Whitney White, with scenic design by Yu-Hsuan Chen, costume design by Andy Jean, lighting design by Cha See, and sound design by Sinan Refik Zafar. The production stage manager was Genevieve Ortiz. The cast was as follows:

ONE / MADE . . . . Rachel Christopher
TWO . . . . Kambi Gathesha
THREE . . . . Alana Raquel Bowers
FOUR / EIGHT . . . . Naomi Lorrain
FIVE / MAN / DRIVER . . . . Beau Thom
SIX / MISS . . . . Ugo Chukwu
SEVEN . . . . Javon Q. Minter
NINE / SONG LEADER . . . . Denise Manning

CHARACTERS

All Black. There may be doubling.

ONE / MADE – W

TWO – M

THREE – W

FOUR – W

FIVE / MAN / DRIVER – M

SIX / MISS – M

SEVEN – M

EIGHT – W

Gender breakdown indicates what has happened in prior productions. I believe it works best if MISS, DRIVER, and MADE are portrayed by participants who identify with these specified gender designations. All other roles are completely fluid.

AUTHOR'S NOTES

This play uses parody and absurdity to confront, to affirm, to celebrate.

The first section is a workshop carried out by the performers. It should be as informal and welcoming as possible. Feel free to improvise the language so that it feels natural.

The second section is experienced more traditionally, with the players presenting memorized text for any observers.

The margins are a space on the periphery of the main playing space. Whenever a figure "disappears," it is into the margins. That is, they remain but are barely visible.

The goal is healing through expression, expulsion, and movement. Have fun but don't play.

First Movement

*(Ideally, anyone viewing the ritual is waiting outside of the playing space. **FOUR** will make the following announcement.)*

FOUR. Welcome everyone.

I'm *[name]* and on behalf of everyone involved I'd like to say that we are really pleased that you've decided to join us. I'd also like to clarify a couple of things before we get started so that everyone understands why we're here.

According to studies, Black people in America are more than twice as likely to be killed by police as white people.

This concerns us.

The officers responsible for these killings often go unpunished.

This concerns us.

Black people must contend with living in a country which continually marginalizes and actively oppresses them. The emotional and physiological toll of this concerns us and is the reason for this ritual.

Let me be clear: this ritual is first and foremost for Black people.

Again. We are glad non-Black people are here. We welcome you but this piece was created and is expressed with Black folks in mind. If you are prepared to honor that through your respectful, conscientious presence, you are welcome to stay.

Parts of the piece you're about to experience are participatory. Whether or not you choose to participate, be respectful. We are very serious about honoring real people who have died and offering strategies for those who need a way to heal.

Please also note that it is not often that Black people have a safe, public space for expressing their unfiltered feelings about anti-Blackness.

We are taking that space today.

Thank you.

>*(As the audience enters the space, they are each offered a black ribbon to pin to their clothing.)*

TWO. Welcome everyone.

The black ribbon symbolizes our grief.

If you'd like a ribbon, please take one, put it on and get into a circle.

If you are someone who is unable to stand for long periods of time, raise your hand and we can grab you a chair.

>*(Once everyone is settled, it continues.)*

Thank you for joining us.

What we are about to carry out is a ritual honoring those lost to racist violence. If at any point during this ritual you find you don't wish to do something that's been asked of you, please step out of the circle. We only ask that you don't disrupt those participating in any way.

Let's start by sharing our names with each other. The way we're going to do it is whoever has this *[name of object – perhaps a candle]* speaks their name, then passes it on to the next person who speaks their name when they've got it.

>*(This happens.)*

Nice to meet you all.

We are here because many of us have been killed, but today in particular we're honoring *[name of person recently killed]* who was killed on *[date of killing]*.

[Name of deceased] was killed by more than the hands of *[pronoun]* killer. *[Name of deceased]* was killed by an idea.

We think it's important to honor *[name of deceased]* and to acknowledge that although *[pronoun]* was killed by this idea, *[pronoun]* was a person of value.

[Name of deceased] lived for *[age of deceased upon death]* years. Let's honor *[pronoun]* by speaking *[pronoun]* name once for each year *[pronoun]* lived.

One

[Name].

Two

[Name].

> *(Others will join. This continues until the number of years the person lived has been reached.)*

This idea, which we believe is partially responsible for the death of *[name of deceased]*, is pretty pervasive in our culture.

It's so pervasive that I'm sure there's someone in this room who has heard someone say something anti-Black.

I'd like us to really consider that.

If you've ever heard someone say something racist about Black people firsthand, please step into the center of the circle.

> *(This happens.)*

Good. Try and have a moment of awareness about who around you has stepped forward and who hasn't as we go through this exercise. Take a moment. Good. You can step back.

If there's anyone here who has ever seen someone be denied something: a promotion, an opportunity to speak, or acknowledgement, for example.

If you've ever witnessed someone being denied something and you believe it was because they are Black, please step forward.

> *(This happens. A moment of suspension, time to reflect on this.)*

Good.

Now, anyone who has ever felt they themselves have been denied something because you are Black, an opportunity to speak, a fair contract, proper medical care, please step forward.

> *(This happens same as before.)*

Now, let's talk about physical safety. Has anyone here ever seen someone physically threatened or assaulted and feel that it was because they were Black? If so, step forward.

> *(This happens same as before.)*

If you've been physically threatened or assaulted and you believe it was because you are Black, step forward.

Now let's get even more specific, since the use of weapons by officers of the law has been such a big part of the conversation lately.

Have you ever seen someone be threatened or actually attacked by an officer of the law with some kind of weapon, a nightstick, a taser, pepper spray or a gun and believe they wouldn't have been treated this way had they not been Black, step into the center.

You can step out.

Now if you yourself have been at the other end of a nightstick, pepper spray, a gun being wielded at you by an officer of the law and feel that being Black had something to do with it, please step into the center.

You can step out.

Now, let's each share one word that describes how we feel in this moment.

It can be any word you'd like to share.

We'll go around the circle passing this *[name of object]* again. Speak your word when it comes to you. Feel free to say "pass" if you wish.

> *(This happens.)*

Let's sit with that for a moment.

Now, we'll do the same thing, but this time we're going to share with each other a word that describes how we'd like to feel in this moment. We've said how we feel, now let's say how we would like to feel.

> *(They pass the object, speaking their word.)*

Good.

Now, again, we're here to do many things, including celebrate the inherent value, the humanity of Black people since we are quite often dehumanized.

With this in mind, we'd like to extend an invitation to you.

Anyone here who feels they have some kind words they'd like to share with a Black person living in an anti-Black society, take a moment to write them down. Take a few moments to do this.

Please be respectful. Do no further harm.

If you don't want to or can't for any reason, no one will give you a hard time.

We invite you to use this as a time for quiet reflection with yourself.

Once you've finished, please place them in this receptacle. *(References receptacle.)*

> *(They're given time to do this. Someone comes around with pens/small bits of paper and the receptacle. The completed notes are placed in the receptacle.)*

When I get frustrated about these things, I find it really helpful to let it out with a yell. So, right now we're going to share a group yell as a strategy for releasing some

of our negative feelings about the untimely death of
[name of deceased] together as a community. It can last
as long as it needs to. As long as one of us is yelling, it's
still happening. You can even take a breath and keep
yelling if you need to. Close your eyes. On the count of
three. One, two, three...

> *(Group yell happens. A beat after.)*

Good. Breath is a great equalizer, isn't it? We all need
to take it to stay alive. Each of us is making use of it as
I speak these words. Right now as a community unique
to this very moment, let's take a collective breath on the
count of three. One, two, three.

> *(They do.)*

Let's do that again.

> *(They do.)*

And one last time.

> *(They do.)*

Now, some of us are going to continue with another
part of the ritual but we need your help getting there.
In order to launch us into the next part of this thing, we
need song, a bridge between this moment and our next.
You could think of this song as fuel.
We're going to teach it to you and we hope that you'll
join us in singing it.
Here we go.

> *(**EIGHT** teaches song.)*

EIGHT.

> SUN COME UP
> SHINE ON ME
> CAN'T STOP IT
> FEELIN FREE
>
> AND I GOT THAT LOVE
> FROM BELOW AND ABOVE
> FROM THE LEFT AND RIGHT

ON EVERY SIDE
WANNA THANK YOU
WANNA THANK YOU
WANNA THANK YOU...

> *(Once it's been learned...)*

TWO. Good, we've got it down.

Now, let's join hands and sing it all together as a way to honor *[name of lost one]*, our community and our cause.

> *(They sing through it twice. As everyone sings, the members of the ensemble begin to drift away, preparing for the next part of the ritual. When it feels right, **TWO** speaks...)*

Let's keep singing as we make our way to our seats.

> *(Once the viewers are seated, **TWO** resumes.)*

The People are coming because it is the day after or the day before it has gone down.

You know what I mean by "it," right?
"It" equals some terrible thing.
Some bang-bang thing.
Some wrong color thing.
The shit that don't stop.

Since it don't stop
we are always before and after it going down.
You feel me?
It happened yesterday and it will happen tomorrow.
We find ourselves between the happenings.

Stay with me.

It is the year *[date and year]* and we are right here in *[name of theater/space/side of town]*.
But it is also circa 1900, in some unknown city in these united states,
what's left of the unknown "negro" propped up
in an old wooden chair

the insides of his head outside
the outsides of his head caved inside
and it is also May 16, 1916 in Waco, Texas, the smell still smelling
and it is of course September 30, 1919 in Arkansas, the screams still slicing through the air.

You get the picture.

The shame of the picture, plus the fuckery of shit having gone down and the knowing that it will go down again will not allow for the mincing of words or giving of too many fucks about delicate sensibilities or convention.

It don't make sense, so why should it make sense?

On your marks

Get set

Bang!

> (**EIGHT** *beats a rhythm into her chest as she sings.*)

EIGHT.
> MAMA HAD A ROSEBUSH IN THE GARDEN
> DADDY HAD A SHIP THAT SAILED THE SEA
> I'M LOOKIN ALL AROUND FOR WHAT I'M HOLDIN
> DON'T SEE NOTHING BUT ME
>
> ME ON THE SIDEWALK, ME ON THE FENCE
> AM I GOIN CRAZY, IT DON'T MAKE NO SENSE
> SEARCHIN FOR THAT GARDEN UNDERGROUND
> WENT HUNTING FOR THAT HIDDEN TREASURE – ALMOST
>   DROWNED
>
> MAMA WHERE'D YOU HIDE THAT ROSEBUSH
> DADDY WHY'D YOU SINK THAT SHIP
> I GOT NOTHIN TO PUT IN MY JEWELRY BOX
> AND I'M FEELIN A LITTLE SICK

ALL.
> O

EIGHT.
> MAMA WON'T YOU TAKE MY TEMPERATURE
> DADDY WON'T YOU FILL THIS SCRIPT

TRYNA GET WELL, TRYNA GET WELL
BEFORE I ABSOLUTELY LOSE MY SHHHHHH –

> *(As the other performers hurry into the margins, the actors portraying* **MADE**, **MAN**, *and* **MISS** *transform into their respective characters.* **MADE** *wears an apron,* **MAN** *wears a limo driver's hat.* **MISS** *may put on a hat and pearls, etc. The tempo of* Fixing Miss *must be clipped. Vaudeville-esque.)*

TWO. The People prepare to say what needs saying.

MADE. Fixing Miss: A play within a play.

Characters: Made, that's "M-A-D-E" – a woman of her own devising. Made stands at a table, sharpening a knife.

MAN. Man. A man weary of the margins. He stands at attention.

MISS. Miss enters. She is white and has a southern dialect not unlike Paula Deen's. She is old and generally jittery.

MAN. As soon as Miss enters, Man becomes Driver, breaking his stillness to tend to her. Driver performs Miss's favorite negro dialect:

Miss, Miss, whatchoo need, Miss? I gotchoo, Miss. Anythang you missed, I'ma get for ya, Miss. Whatcha need?

MISS. I don't need anything from you.

I am wealthy and white and liberated.

My hands are clean.

I am wealthy and white

So wealthy and white that I don't need anything from you.

DRIVER. But...uh, Miss, I'll do anything for to make you happy! Thas what I'm here for!

MISS. O, hush up.

DRIVER. I needs me some purpose, Miss.

MISS. *(Enjoying this.)* O, stop.

DRIVER. I could frame ya if ya want. Black is a real good color for a frame. I can do anything to make ya feel good about yoself. It'd be my privilege –

MISS. "Privilege"? Don't you start about privilege. Why, I've worked for everything I've ever gotten.

DRIVER. Yes'm...what I mean is I'm real happy to be some kinda vehicle fo yo edificamation. I needs my purpose up in this here play, otherwise I'm jus gon slide right offa the character list and into the margins, and I doan wanna do that!

MISS. Not my problem.

DRIVER. I means it, Miss, I means it! Gimme somethin to do!

MISS. What you do with yourself is none of my concern. My hands are clean.

(**DRIVER** *bends over backward.*)

DRIVER. I'll bend over backward! See! See! See!

MISS. You are making a fool of yourself –

(**DRIVER** *begins to slide into the margins.*)

DRIVER. Please! Please! I'm bein sucked into the margins, Miss!

(**MISS** *watches him go. A moment. Then:*)

MISS. O, alright. Come on back.

(**DRIVER** *is back in a flash.*)

DRIVER. Thank you, Miss!

MISS. I spose I could use a seat.

(**DRIVER** *happily gets on all fours. She sits on him.*)

But don't think this means I need you. I can get rid of you whenever I please. You are a luxury.

DRIVER. Yes'm.

MISS. My hands are clean.

DRIVER. Yes'm.

MISS. *(Quietly.)* You don't steal, do you?

DRIVER. No'm.

MISS. Good. Calling you out for stealing would make me look mean and racist and I am neither mean nor racist. What I am is wealthy, white and liberated.

DRIVER. 'Course you is.

MISS. My hands are clean.

DRIVER. Yes'm.

MISS. Now take me over to the maid.

DRIVER. *(Forgetting "negro dialect.")* Shall I sing a negro spiritual as I do?

MISS. What?

DRIVER. Shall I sing a –

MISS. I don't understand a word you're saying.

DRIVER. *(Back to "negro dialect.")* I mean, you be wantin me to sing one of my colored songs, Missus, while I be carryin you around? We real good at makin music!

MISS. No. Your shucking and jiving and driving are sufficient.

DRIVER. He carries her to Made.

MADE. Who is still sharpening the knife.

MISS. What are you doing?

MADE. Kneading flour.

MISS. O. Making fresh bread, are we?

MADE. Yes, we are.

MISS. Hm.

> *(She taps* **DRIVER** *and he carries her away.)*

Did you hear that?

DRIVER. Yes'm.

MISS. She was a bit impudent, wasn't she?

DRIVER. Yes'm.

MISS. And I'm not entirely sure about that bread she's making. I am gluten-free, you know, and I am certain she is not taking care to remove all of the gluten.

DRIVER. You prolly right.

MISS. You can't pull one over on me. I am a friend to your kind but that does not make me a fool.

DRIVER. No'm. It don't.

MISS. That look in her eyes was very telling.

DRIVER. What did it tell you, Miss?

MISS. Something about fire, a school house and ghosts. That mean anything to you?

DRIVER. No'm. But –

MISS. I try to understand the struggle. I see the movies. I saw the *Django Unchained* and *The Help*, *The Butler*, the *Selma*, the *I Am Not Your Negro* and the *Black Panther* to boot.

DRIVER. Yes'm –

MISS. And I have Black friends. We're friends, aren't we?

DRIVER. Tha besta friends. You lets me listen to all your troubles.

MISS. You are not slaves. You work of your own free will.

DRIVER. Yes'm. Y'all let us do whatever we want. White House or jail house or –

MISS. Your choice.

DRIVER. Yes'm. And issa privilege to be up under you –

MISS. What's that? Privilege? I am not some trust fund ninny I have worked for everything that is mine Privilege had nothing to do with it! Now take me over to the maid! I want to non-racistly assert myself as her boss but not as a racist.

DRIVER. Yes'm. Dis here yo story –

He carries her over to Made.

MADE. Who is now loading a bow and arrow.

MISS. Hello there.

Hi.

Hi?

       (**MISS** *looks to* **DRIVER** *for help. He shrugs.*)

How-what-how's your day going?

MADE. Fine.

MISS. What are you up to?

MADE. Laundry.

MISS. O. That's nice.

Why are you doing laundry at this hour?

MADE. Why not?

MISS. Well, it's a strange hour for laundry. Wouldn't you like to take tea with me? We could talk about our kids. I'm sure they've got lots in common.

MADE. I don't have any kids.

MISS. Really?

MADE. Really.

MISS. Are you planning on having –

MADE. If you don't mind, I'm needed doing this laundry.

MISS. Well. I do mind. I'm trying to have a conversation with you. Get to know you. You've been employed here for quite some time and I think we should become acquainted, so put that laundry down and let's talk.

MADE. We can talk but I can't stop with this laundry.

MISS. Fine. Well. I'll start.

I enjoy brunch. And church and my work, which is the care of children. All kinds of children.

You?

Ahem.

What do you like –

MADE. I really don't want to mess up and put the lights with the darks. If you'll excuse me.

MISS. I-I-okay.

> *(Pats* **DRIVER**, *who takes her away.)*

I am troubled. This is troubling.

I think I'll have to let her go.

DRIVER. O.

MISS. What?

DRIVER. Huh?

MISS. You –

DRIVER. Whah?

MISS. What's that?

DRIVER. Nothin –

MISS. Well?

DRIVER. Naw –

MISS. I –

DRIVER. Nuh-uh –

MISS. What do you mean by saying that? Am I to keep an insolent worker?

DRIVER. No'm, but –

MISS. Am I to put up with someone who can't be bothered to make friends with me?

I do wonder what, if you'll pardon the expression, crawled up her butt!

I am a friend to you all but that does not mean that I have to tolerate sass!

I non-racistly assert the right to have whichever colored maid I like!

DRIVER. Yes'm.

MISS. What?

DRIVER. Nothin.

MISS. Do you –

DRIVER. No'm –

MISS. What's that look about? I don't owe her anything. Take me back over there right this instant!

DRIVER. You da boss!

MISS. Wait! I'm not going anywhere.

Ahem.

You. Maid. What are you doing?

MADE. Made is oiling a machete. She does not even look at Miss.

(*To* **MISS**.) Sweeping.

MISS. Put down that broom and come here.

MADE. I'm needed sweeping.

MISS. You are needed where I say you are needed I can do my own sweeping I grew up doing my own sweeping I never needed anyone to do it for me I grew up poor You are a luxury My hands are clean Please come over here.

MADE. Made goes to Miss, hips first.

MISS. Your sass of late has become too much for me to handle It's just gotten out of hand Too much Way overboard. Have you got anything to say for yourself?

MADE. Made answers with her shoulders. *(A shrug.)*

MISS. Are you going through some sort of private crisis –

MADE. Nope.

MISS. If you were having some issue –

MADE. Nope –

MISS. I understand and am sympathetic –

MADE. No issue –

MISS. Maybe one of your kids is sick –

>   *(**MADE** slaps **MISS**.)*

MADE. Made slaps the shit out of Miss.

>   *(**MISS** continues as if she hadn't noticed.)*

MISS. Maybe one of your kids is sick and you're needing some time off –

>   *(**MADE** slaps **MISS** again. Again, **MISS** continues
>   as if she hadn't noticed.)*

You're needing some time off to tend to your little ones. I can understand that.

MADE. I don't have any fucking kids you witless cunt! Made punches Miss.

>   *(Punches, but **MISS** isn't affected. She shakes
>   her head, confused.)*

MISS. You seem upset.

MADE. Made cannot stop hitting Miss.

>   *(**MISS** looks to **DRIVER**, who shrugs his
>   shoulders.)*

MISS. You must be having a bad day –

> (**MADE** *kisses* **MISS** *squarely on the mouth.*
> **MISS** *mimes the action and describes it, dying
> a hilarious, dramatic death:*)

Miss is horrified, reacts as if she's been shot, stabbed,
punched. She screams, moans, and rages, ending up on
the floor.

You –

You –

You! Are! Fired!!

> (**MISS** *is very still.*)

MADE & MAN. O. Shit.

> (**THREE** *enters from the margins with a bowl
> filled with shredded white paper. She drops
> bits of the paper on the ground as she speaks,
> moving throughout the space.*)

THREE. Do you remember when I tried to love you?
You and you stood with me in a circle at a party
on a boat, in a roaring house by a fire
in a log cabin and we breathed the same air but not
really
yours seemed bigger and though I stood with you and
you in that tight circle
you and you let a truth tumble out of your mouth
which put me in Africa with a bone in my nose
doing a nigger dance
which put me in The Ghetto looking suspicious
and being suspiciously quite nigger-ly
you and you put me beneath your boots
or in the cupboard or in the corner of your eyes,
platoon, spelling bee –

> (**FOUR** *and* **EIGHT** *appear. They are standing
> in a bathroom mirror at a bar.*)

EIGHT. So, I tried to, like, be cool about it, you know.

Ever since I read that psychotherapy book, I'm all into my breath and checking in with my body and stuff, you know?

FOUR. I feel you.

EIGHT. But he was pissed. You know that really special nobody-ever-dares-call-me-on-my-bullshit, especially-not-some-negro-wench way white men get pissed?

FOUR. I know it very well.

EIGHT. So, I'm going in like I do, tryna explain things calmly, you know –

FOUR. O, Lord. What'd he say?

EIGHT. He looked at me and said...
He doesn't see color...

> *(They freak out, running all over the room, laughing. Maybe they "shout," à la a person stricken with the Holy Ghost or they twerk incredulously or some amused/shocked expression of "Lord, help me not to slap somebody.")*

FOUR. No the hell he didn't.

EIGHT. Yes the hell he did.

FOUR. No, his ass didn't.

EIGHT. Yes, his ass did.

FOUR. What'd you say?

EIGHT. I didn't say anything.

FOUR. Nothing?

EIGHT. What could I say?

FOUR. I can think of a few things.

EIGHT. Nah. I'm tired. I just politely leaned forward in my chair...

FOUR. Mm-hm.

EIGHT. And took his mouth.

FOUR. What?

EIGHT. Off his face. I removed his mouth.

FOUR. You took his mouth off his face?

EIGHT. Yes.

FOUR. You removed your coworker's mouth from his face?

EIGHT. I did, indeed. From right between his nose and his chin.

FOUR. You removed your white coworker's mouth-girl-what-how-how?

EIGHT. I just...

>   (*She demonstrates snatching a mouth off of someone's face with one hand.*)

Now he out here mouthless.

FOUR. Giiirrrrrrl –

>   (**SIX** *rises, no longer* **MISS**. *He and* **FIVE** *– no longer* **MAN** *– speak.*)

FIVE. Why do you keep fucking with these white people?

SIX. What do you mean?

FIVE. You fuck with them.

SIX. I fux with everybody.

FIVE. You tryna be funny?

SIX. Maybe.

FIVE. Do you want to die?

SIX. C'mon –

FIVE. You do, don't you?

SIX. Is that a real question?

FIVE. You have a death wish.

SIX. Suicide by white person. Is that a thing?

FIVE. I'm serious.

SIX. Chill, bruh. They fuck with me and I respond in kind.

FIVE. If you don't want to die, quit responding! And quit walking down the street.

SIX. You don't want me to walk down the street?

FIVE. No.

SIX. I can't walk down the street?

FIVE. No, you can't.

Especially not with the way you walk down the street.

SIX. The way?

FIVE. Yes, the way.

SIX. And what way is that?

FIVE. You know.

SIX. I don't. I'm curious. Like, how do I do it?

FIVE. Brazenly.

In their neighborhoods.

Brazenly!

You know they hate that.

SIX. But show me though. Show me how I do it.

FIVE. You do it all like this.

> (**FIVE** *imitates* **SIX** *walking down a street. It is a normal walk.*)

SIX. Like that? That's how I do it?

FIVE. That's exactly how you do it!

SIX. O, 'cause I thought I was more like...

> (**SIX** *does this ridiculous pimp-daddy walk, complete with gang signs and maybe even ends with a jailhouse pose.*)

I thought that was how I did it.

FIVE. No, no. You definitely do it like this:

> (**FIVE** *demonstrates the normal walk again.*)

And then you be all like,

"Hi." Like that. Like y'all are pals.

SIX. We're not pals?

FIVE. No. You and white people are not pals.

SIX. Homies?

FIVE. No.

SIX. Confidants –

FIVE. God. No!

SIX. Alright! Damn.

> (**SEVEN** *appears.*)

SEVEN. Daddy used to say,

"*[Name of actor]*, you don't get to be foolish, too, boy.
You already Black. Don't add Fool to the equation.
Foolish Black folks get swept off their feet in the worst way.
Foolish Black folks get cheated out of their own skin and bone.
Foolish Black folk come to this world like rabbits
and get taken out like trash.
Black and foolish is the last thing you wanna be.
You can be uppity, you can be stoic but you bet not, bet not be foolish."
So, Fool ain't in me.
Uh-uh.
It ain't in my food, my walk or my attire.
You will not find Fool in the gin I drink,
under my fingernails or in my speech.
Let them be foolish
I am very Black and very much the picture of perfection
I keeps it sharp.
If you say you seen Fool anywhere on *[name of actor]*'s person,
you. a muthafuckin. lie.

> (**FOUR** *enters the space, holding a bowl of shredded white paper.*)

FOUR. When I say "Black people," I want you to say, "Yeah."
Black people.

ALL. Yeah.

FOUR. Black people.

ALL. Yeah.

FOUR. Black people.

ALL. Yeah!

FOUR. A lot of times when people call your name like that, a lot of times when they say "Black" they're saying something bad about you.
Am I right, Black people?

ALL. Yeah.

FOUR. Big Black people.

ALL. Yeah.

FOUR. Loud Black people.

ALL. Yeah.

FOUR. Angry Black people.

ALL. Yeah.

FOUR. Stupid Black people.

ALL. Yeah.

FOUR. Ugly Black people.

ALL. Yeah.

FOUR. Poor Black people.

ALL. Yeah.

FOUR. Criminal Black people.

ALL. Yeah.

FOUR. AIDS-havin Black people.

ALL. Yeah.

FOUR. Fat Black people.

ALL. Yeah.

FOUR. Lazy Black people.

ALL. Yeah.

FOUR. Ghetto Black people.

ALL. Yeah.

FOUR. Urban (Black people).

ALL. Yeah.

FOUR. Sassy Black people.

ALL. Yeah.

FOUR. Entitled-ass Black people.

ALL. Yeah.

FOUR. Not even worth mentioning Black people.

ALL. Yeah.

FOUR. Synonymous with "slave" Black people.

ALL. Yeah.

FOUR. You best behave Black people.

ALL. Yeah.

FOUR. Dead Black people.

ALL. Yeah.

FOUR. Dead for bein Black Black people.

ALL. Yeah.

FOUR. Your bodies are dangerous Black people.

ALL. Yeah.

FOUR. You are walking weapons Black people.

ALL. Yeah.

FOUR. You got some weight on you Black people.

ALL. Yeah.

FOUR. You ready to unpack Black people?

ALL. Yeah.

FOUR. Drop somethin!

> *(They drop bits of paper slowly as* **THREE** *enters, dropping more paper.)*

THREE. You lookin at me like, "what?"

You lookin at me like "whoa"

Like "whoa" Like "what" Like "whoa"

What

What

What

When so many words are fighting their way out of my mouth that it foams

You and you don't want to listen to the words themselves preferring, instead, to ponder the foam's density and viscosity like, "Where did it come from? Why she so mad?"

Well, I just don't know.

I guess there was a sale on Mad down at the Mad Store

So I went down and bought me some Mad

And, here it is.

Meanwhile, I and I can't find myself in the mirror, in the reflection of the screen

unless of course I am biting myself
You and you approve of the biting of the self
especially when it is a self that looks like me
You love it, O, you love it when I bite myself
because that is the kind of Black story you like.
When I am heavy and downtrodden
with biting myself
when I wear the flavor of Blackness you like
When it is warm and fuzzy Blackness that does not
creep under your bedroom door at night
Blackness that does not disrupt brunch or make you
question
the things your privilege steals and steals from me
O, you love it
You wield your pen
I blubber most Blackly
You nod your head, you know this story
I weep, I moan, I reach for you from down below
You love it
You wield your pen most bravely
You are afraid to come to my neighborhood
You would never help my aunt with her groceries
You do not see me coming
but you come see my story
You sit in your soft chair
You review me and you do not feel the foolishness of it
You feel no shame
You really think you are in charge
I'd be embarrassed for you if I weren't so busy fighting
for my life
If I were to turn my teeth toward you
If I were to turn my teeth toward you
You and you would not know what to do and do
Do you do you
Do you remember when I tried to love you?

Do you remember when I tried to love you?
It was like riding a bike without a chain.

FIVE. Brazenly.

SIX. What?

FIVE. You walk around in their neighborhoods.
Brazenly!
You know they hate that.

SIX. Not their neighborhoods.
Not their streets.
Everything they got, they stole.
Streets and people
Streets and people
But they ain't got me.

FIVE. If they got guns, they got you.

SIX. Naw.

FIVE. The judge and the senators they got.

SIX. Naw.

FIVE. The police, they got.
Time and the law, they got.
They got you.

SIX. Naw.

FIVE. You keep on. You'll find out.

SIX. Whatever.

(**SIX** *makes to leave.*)

FIVE. Where you going?

SIX. To one of "their" houses.

FIVE. Don't be stupid.

SIX. Gotta take a leak. Gonna water the azaleas.

FIVE. That isn't funny. Stop laughing.

SIX. A brotha can't even laugh?

FIVE. You don't have to do it the way you do it.
In their faces
loud and wide
showing all your teeth

you laugh like –

SIX. You're right, I do.

But those crackas deserve it.

FIVE. O my god, you must really want to die.

SEVEN. So when they shoot another one of us, I come up with a plan.

I get a razor and cut a straight line, not too deep, just deep enough to do the trick.

I cut from the navel to the sternum

and then two more lines from the sternum out to the shoulders.

A "Y"

like how they cut the dead ones open.

I figure if I already look dead, there ain't nothin for them to kill.

Iss like playin possum.

You see? Sharp.

> (**EIGHT** *and* **FOUR** *still before the mirror.*)

EIGHT. Don't look at me like that.

FOUR. A white man's mouth? Just – just like that?

EIGHT. Just took it off his face.

FOUR. O my god! Was anyone else there?

EIGHT. O yeah. Other people were there. My supervisor's jaw hit the floor. They got all wide in the eyes, like "*[Name of actor]*'s gone crazy." I put that mouth in my purse and left.

FOUR. No one tried to stop you?

EIGHT. Now you know good and well they were scared.

FOUR. What does it look like?

EIGHT. Like a little fish flopping around. Look.

> (*She opens her purse but not for long, lest the mouth jump out.*)

FOUR. That's disgusting.

EIGHT. I know. It won't shut up, either.

FOUR. What's it saying?

EIGHT. The usual. Something about my neck.

FOUR. They're gonna come after you. With fire, they'll come.

EIGHT. And I'll be here with this mouth. Let 'em come.

FOUR. Girl.

EIGHT. Tired.

SEVEN. I strut down the street
 with this Y so neat and pretty
 lookin like a muthafuckin superhero.
 Don't need no cape or nothing.
 Naw, don't need no cape.
 All I gotta do is – shit.

> (**SEVEN** *smarts. A sharp pain from the "Y" on his chest.*)

 The fuck?

THREE. I and I beamed my least nigger-ly smile and offered you a beer
 and you took the beer but would not let our fingers touch
 I pretended not to notice –
 bigger-ing my non-nigger smile but you got scared
 or horny
 You told me, you tell me a story
 about someone you love who hates me
 You say,
 "My uncle is a bit racist but you must understand that he is from a different time" and so the arrowhead is in me
 not you nor your uncle
 me
 I try to take it out gingerly – I try
 This is an office function, after all
 It wouldn't do to walk around with an arrow in my back –

SEVEN. This ain't my Y. This Y's got fresh blood. And it feels like I'm all hollowed out –

THREE. Arrow in my back –

SEVEN. Iss enough ghosts up in here.

> *(All take an audible breath and run to the margins, save for* **TWO**.*)*

Second Movement

> *(This second time around, all action occurs a bit more quickly than the last time.)*

TWO. The People are coming because it is the day after or the day before it has gone down.

You know what I mean by "it," right?

"It" equals some terrible thing.

Some bang-bang thing.

Some wrong color thing.

The shit that don't stop.

Since it don't stop

we are always before and after it going down.

We find ourselves between the happenings.

Stay with me.

It is the year *[date and year]* and we are right here in *[name of theater/space/side of town]*.

And it is also July 19, 1935 in Fort Lauderdale, Florida, the little girls chewing taffy and watching the swing, swing, swing.

And it is also June 16, 1944 in Columbus, South Carolina, the boy going into the death house.

And it is of course August 28, 1955, the Tallahatchie River fuller than usual.

You get the picture.

The shame of the picture, plus the fuckery of shit having gone down and the knowing that it will go down again

will not allow for the giving of too many fucks.

It don't make sense, so why should it make sense?

On your marks

Get set

Bang!

EIGHT.
    ME ON THE SIDEWALK, ME ON THE FENCE

    AM I GOIN CRAZY, IT DON'T MAKE NO SENSE

    SEARCHIN FOR THAT GARDEN UNDERGROUND

    WENT HUNTING FOR THAT HIDDEN TREASURE – ALMOST
        DROWNED

    MAMA WHERE'D YOU HIDE THAT ROSEBUSH

    DADDY WHY'D YOU SINK THAT SHIP

    I GOT NOTHIN TO PUT IN MY JEWELRY BOX

    AND I'M FEELIN A LITTLE SICK

ALL.
    O

EIGHT.
    MAMA WON'T YOU TAKE MY TEMPERATURE

    DADDY WON'T YOU FILL THIS SCRIPT

    TRYNA GET WELL, TRYNA GET WELL

    BEFORE I ABSOLUTELY LOSE MY SHHHHHH –

        (The other performers hurry into the margins
        as the actors portraying **MADE, MAN,** *and*
        MISS *reset for the beginning of the following*
        section. The tempo of Fixing Miss *must be*
        even more clipped and the performances
        more intensified.)

TWO. The People prepare to say it.

MADE. Fixing Miss: A play within a play.

    Characters: "M-A-D-E" – a woman of her own devising.
    Made stands at a table loading a revolver.

MAN. Man. A man weary of the margins. Flexible. He stands
    at attention.

MISS. Miss enters. She is white, pearls, pantsuit, degrees, jittery.

MAN. As soon as Miss enters, Man becomes Driver, performing Miss's favorite negro dialect: Miss, Miss, whatcha need, Miss? Anythang you missed, I'ma get for ya, Miss. Whatcha need?

MISS. Don't need anything from you.

Liberated and educated.

So liberated and educated that I don't need anything from you.

DRIVER. But…uh, Miss, I'll do anything for to make you happy!

MISS. O, hush.

DRIVER. Need me some purpose –

MISS. O, stop.

DRIVER. I could frame ya, if ya want. I'm frame-colored. It'd be my privilege –

MISS. Don't you start about privilege.

DRIVER. Yes ma'am… I need me a purpose up in this here play, otherwise I'm jus gonna slide right off the character list and into the margins –

MISS. Not my problem.

DRIVER. I mean it, Miss. Gimme somethin to do!

MISS. None of my concern.

(**DRIVER** *begins to slide into the margins.*)

DRIVER. I'm bein sucked into the margins, Miss!

(**MISS** *watches him go. A moment. Then:*)

MISS. O, come on back.

(**DRIVER** *is back in a flash.*)

DRIVER. Thank you, Miss!

MISS. No slouching. Stand up straight.

(*He does so.*)

Not too straight.

DRIVER. Huh?

MISS. Just. Please. My feet are tired.

>(**DRIVER** *happily gets on all fours. She sits on him.*)

But don't think this means I need you.

DRIVER. Yes ma'am.

MISS. My hands are clean.

DRIVER. Yes ma'am.

MISS. *(Quietly.)* You don't   have a record, do you?

DRIVER. No ma'am.

MISS. Good. Firing you for having a record would make me look mean and racist.

DRIVER. 'Course.

MISS. My hands are clean.

DRIVER. Yes ma'am.

MISS. Now take me over to the housekeeper.

DRIVER. He carries her to Made.

MADE. Who is still loading those bullets into that revolver.

MISS. What are you doing?

MADE. Shelling peas.

MISS. Those don't look like peas. Exotic?

MADE. Yes.

>(**MISS** *taps* **DRIVER** *and he carries her away.*)

MISS. You hear that?

DRIVER. Yes ma'am.

MISS. Bit of an attitude.

DRIVER. Yes ma'am.

MISS. Had an attitude with Mama, too.

DRIVER. Uh-huh.

MISS. And something is not right about those peas.

DRIVER. No ma'am.

MISS. That look in her eyes.

DRIVER. Yup.

MISS. I try my best. I'm one of the good ones.

DRIVER. Yup.

MISS. Should I be treated like trash just because you all have been oppressed?

DRIVER. Uh…?

MISS. My hands are clean.

DRIVER. Sho nuff. You 'bout the nicest white lady –

MISS. Hush. Got to focus. Something's off-kilter here. You feel it?

DRIVER. This yo story –

MISS. Take me back over there. I am going to assert myself non-racistly.

> (**DRIVER** *takes her over to* **MADE**, *who mimes cleaning the chamber of a machine gun.*)

MADE. Made is now cleaning the chamber of a machine gun.

MISS. How-what-how's your day going?

MADE. Fine.

MISS. What are you up to?

MADE. Scrubbing the bathtub.

MISS. Strange hour for scrubbing.
We could talk about our kids. I'm sure they've got lots in common.

MADE. I don't have any kids.

MISS. Really? Mama said you had –

MADE. Really.

MISS. Are you planning on having –

MADE. If you don't mind, I'm needed scrubbing this tub.

MISS. I'm trying to have a conversation with you. You've been in the family for years. Let's talk.

MADE. We can talk but I can't stop scrubbing.

MISS. I'll start.
I enjoy brunch, church and children.
What do you like –

MADE. Don't want to mess up and miss a spot. Excuse me.

MISS. Okay.

>*(Pats **DRIVER**, who takes her away.)*

I'll have to let her go.

DRIVER. O.

MISS. What?

DRIVER. Huh?

MISS. That was –

DRIVER. What –

MISS. Huh?

DRIVER. I don't –

MISS. Am I to keep a maid with an attitude problem?

DRIVER. No ma'am, but –

MISS. I non-racistly assert the right to have whichever one of y'all that I like!

DRIVER. Yes ma'am.

MISS. What?

DRIVER. Nothin.

MISS. Huh?

DRIVER. What?

MISS. She has other options, doesn't she?

DRIVER. Y'all done gave –

MISS. Take me back over there so I can fire her.

DRIVER. You the boss!

MISS. Wait!

Ahem.

You. Housekeeper. What are you doing?

MADE. Made is aiming a rocket launcher. She does not even look at Miss

>Vacuuming.

MISS. Put down that vacuum and come here.

MADE. I'm needed vacuuming.

MISS. You are needed where I say you are needed You are a luxury My hands are clean Come over here.

MADE. Made puts down the rocket launcher.

MISS. Your sass has gotten out of hand. Have you got anything to say?

MADE. What?

MISS. Are you going through a private crisis –

MADE. Nope.

MISS. Having some issue –

MADE. Nope –

MISS. I'm sympathetic –

MADE. No issue –

MISS. Maybe one of your kids is sick –

> (**MADE** *slaps* **MISS**.)

MADE. Made slaps the shit out of Miss.

> (**MISS** *continues as if she hadn't noticed.*)

MISS. Maybe one of your kids is sick and –

> (**MADE** *slap* **MISS** *again. Again,* **MISS** *continues as if she hadn't noticed.*)

You're needing some time off. I can understand that.

MADE. I don't have any fucking kids you witless cunt!

MISS. You seem upset. If you'll apologize for your attitude today –

MADE. Made cannot stop!

> (**MADE** *continues hitting* **MISS**, *to no avail.*)

MISS. Woman troubles, I presume. Not making use of one's womb will do that to –

> (**MADE** *kisses* **MISS** *square on the mouth.*)

Miss is horrified, reacts as if she's been shot, stabbed, punched. She screams, moans, and rages, ending up on the floor.

You –

You –

You! Are! Fired!!

> (**MISS** *is dead.*)

MADE & MAN. O. shit.

THREE. I tried to love you, I tried.

I tried to laugh with you but it sounded wrong.

It was all jittery. It was all jittery because of your joke about how many Black people it takes to screw in a light bulb or how all the Black girls dance or whatever funny joke they're telling about Black people these days.

I looked down and realized joke was on me

literally, all over me

and in me.

The kids were laughing. All of their pink faces laughing.

Teacher was trying to hide a titter behind her hand.

I do a little dance as I run back to the ghetto hoping I don't look too suspicious or particularly ready to die –

EIGHT. You were right about them coming

You were right and now

Won't nothing straighten out my neck

Can't seem to

Straighten out my neck

Took a crane to it.

FOUR. Prayed.

EIGHT. Took a hammer to it.

FOUR. Prayed.

EIGHT. Got a brace for it. Wept and wailed.

FOUR. Prayed.

EIGHT. Got on the news and shook the man's hand.

Said it was okay, was gonna be okay.

FOUR. Told people to pray.

Stopped the blood from coming out of my lover's body with my mouth.

Plugged it up.

EIGHT & FOUR. The camera rolling the whole time.

EIGHT. My spine doesn't riot, my arms aren't raised.

FOUR. Held hands with the other mothers.

Pinned a flower to me.

EIGHT. Picked up the baby and the entrails they cut out
All in the dust. Picked them up.

FOUR. Took the thing from 'round my neck –

EIGHT. And ankles.

FOUR. You ever try to kiss someone but you can't 'cause
you're too crooked?

EIGHT. Yeah. All the time. My ex used to tell me I tasted
like copper.

FOUR. How does he know what copper tastes like?

EIGHT. Girrrrrrrrrrl.

SEVEN. This ain't my Y.
Somebody else did this one.
This Y is bleeding like a fresh cut.
This Y got stitches in it.
And I can't find my insides.
I'm missing my insides like how the dead ones is
missing their insides –

FIVE. You fux with white people?

SIX. Huh?

FIVE. With white people. You fux with them?

SIX. Naw, homey. Well. From time to time.

FIVE. Why?

SIX. Why?

FIVE. Yeah, why?

SIX. 'Cause all god's children needs to be fucked with.

(They laugh.)

FIVE. How do you fuck with them?

SIX. Like this.

(He walks normally.)

FIVE. You do that?

SIX. Hell yeah!

FIVE. In public?

SIX. Hell, hell yeah.

FIVE. You crazy.
   You got white friends?

SIX. Eyup.

FIVE. For real?

SIX. Eyup.

FIVE. How many?

SIX. I got so many white friends.

FIVE. How many?

SIX. Like seventy-eight.

FIVE. You actually keep count?

SIX. Eyup.

FIVE. What do you do with your white friends?

SIX. Go to the mall, eat biscotti, play video games.

FIVE. For real?

SIX. Yeah. Why you making such a big deal? I do the same
   thing with them I do with anyone else.

FIVE. For real?

SIX. Eyup.

FIVE. Go to their houses?

SIX. Eyup.

FIVE. What do you do there?

SIX. We watch movies. About elephants.

FIVE. Do you talk?

SIX. Only when the channel needs to be changed.

FIVE. O. That sounds normal.

SIX. And when my friend reaches down for a bit of popcorn
   but accidentally eats a bit of my finger.

FIVE. Say what?

SIX. Sometimes she eats but doesn't know she's eating me,
   so I'll be like, "Hey, Katelyn. You're eating me." If she
   hears me, she stops.

FIVE. O. That sounds normal.

SEVEN. Am
   Am I?

Y'all, am I d–

(He would've said "dead.")

FOUR. Black people.

ALL. Yeah.

FOUR. Black people.

ALL. Yeah.

FOUR. Black people.

ALL. Yeah.

FOUR. We're gonna get in so much trouble for being gathered together like this, Black people.

ALL. Yeah.

FOUR. And we ain't even in church, Black people.

ALL. Yeah.

FOUR. And yelling, Black people.

ALL. Yeah.

FOUR. And mad in public, Black people.

ALL. Yeah.

FOUR. They might drop a nuke, Black people.

ALL. Yeah.

FOUR. In fact, I'm sure they are, Black people.

ALL. Yeah.

FOUR. I can hear the bomb coming.

You'd better leave something behind before it gets here! Drop something!

> *(**FOUR** and/or **THREE** and/or anyone else with shredded paper drops some.)*

THREE. They're all like, "What's the problem, *[own name]*?"

'Cause as far as they're concerned, there isn't one.

Which of course is a little maddening.

I mean, just talking about it makes me feel like I'm orbiting them.

I don't want to orbit. I don't want to orbit.

What are they, the Sun? O god, it is maddening.

I tried to love, I tried.
It was like falling and waiting for the bottom
waiting for the bottom.
You know it's going to come
But when?

SEVEN. O, shit.
There's someone
someone's behind me. Shit.
Following me?

> (**SEVEN** *walks swiftly to escape his pursuer.*)

FIVE. But...

SIX. But?

FIVE. But what if she doesn't hear you?

SIX. Who? My friend?

FIVE. Yeah, what if your friend doesn't hear you say, "Hey, Katelyn. You're eating me." And doesn't stop eating you. What do you do next?

SIX. Well.
I usually just eat a little of myself. So she doesn't feel embarrassed.

FIVE. O.

SIX. Just a little of myself, you know?

FIVE. Yeah. Okay. That sounds normal –

SEVEN. O, he's definitely following me. Definitely.

EIGHT. You ever get your neck fixed?

FOUR. No. But now the world is bent too, so it all evens out.

EIGHT. Damn.

SEVEN. But I don't know why he's following me.
I got this Y in me
This deep Y in me
I look like one of the dead ones
I might *be* one of the so I don't know what else he want –

THREE. I tried. Try. Past and present. I mean, I really, really do and did.

I beam, I smile, I listen. I do not take offense.

This is an office function, after all.

This is a classroom, after all.

This is a production meeting, after all –

SEVEN. I don't know what else he want.

I don't know what else he want –

THREE. This is a play, after all –

SEVEN. Iss enough ghosts up in here –

> *(All take an audible breath and rush into the margins, save for* **TWO**.*)*

Third Movement

> *(This third time around, all action occurs a bit more quickly than the last time. Damn near breakneck speed.)*

TWO. The People are coming because it is the day after or the day before it has gone down.

You know what I mean by "it," right?

The shit that don't stop.

It is the year *[date and year]* and we are right here in *[name of theater/space/side of town]*.

And it is September 10, 2014 in Utah, the questions still looming.

And June 17, 2015 in Charleston, the bodies still smoking.

And July 5, 2016, the boy still wailing for his daddy.

And July 6, 2016, the moan moaning and the red stain staining.

And July 20, 2018, the papa still pleading.

And today, the people still trying to be people when it seems it might be easier to be something else.

Get it?

Bang!

EIGHT.
> MAMA WHERE'D YOU HIDE THAT ROSEBUSH
> DADDY WHY'D YOU SINK THAT SHIP
> I GOT NOTHIN TO PUT IN MY JEWELRY BOX
> AND I'M FEELIN A LITTLE SICK

ALL.
> O
>
> MAMA WON'T YOU TAKE MY TEMPERATURE
> DADDY WON'T YOU FILL THIS SCRIPT
> TRYNA GET WELL, TRYNA GET WELL
> BEFORE I ABSOLUTELY LOSE MY SHHHHHH –

> Shh sh sh
> Shh sh sh
> Shh sh sh.

> > *(The tempo of* Fixing Miss *this time around must be really fast, as if the players are acting on fast-forward. The characterizations are angrier and the most realistic we've seen them. We see and feel their frustration with having to repeat themselves.)*

TWO. The People prepare –

MADE. Fixing Miss: Play within play.
Characters: Made. Fed up.

MAN. Man. Weary of the margins. At attention.

MISS. Miss enters. White. Jittery.

MAN. Whatchoo need?

MISS. Nothing from you. Liberated.

MAN. Needs me some purpose –

MISS. Not my problem.

MAN. Characters in plays need purpose.

MISS. Not my problem.

MAN. Prolly gonna die.

MISS. Sounds like an exaggeration.

MAN. No, I'm actually afraid that I'm going to die –

MISS. Not my problem, nor my fault. Liberated. Could use a seat, though.

MAN. He becomes a seat.

MISS. Miss see The Help.
Who's that?

MAN. That's *[name of actor portraying* **MADE***]*.

MISS. What's her deal?

MAN. She might be tired.

MISS. Of what?

MAN. Let's ask her.

MISS. You there, come here.

MADE. Made looks to the audience. Who's she talking to?

MISS. Miss asks Driver,
Who's she talking to?

MAN. I don't know. Lotta ghosts around here –

MISS. Miss asks the Help who she's talking to.

MADE. No one. Everyone.

MISS. Come here.

MADE. I'm busy.

MISS. I said come here.

MADE. Okay. I'll come.
If you get my name right.

MISS. If I what?

MADE. Get my name right. What's my name?

MISS. How am I to know?

MADE. He just told you.

MISS. Did he?

MAN. I did.

MISS. Well. You must be *[name of female cast member not playing* **MADE***]*.

> *(That cast member speaks up from wherever they are onstage.)*

CAST MEMBER 1. No. That's me.

MISS. Uh, okay. Then you must be *[name of another female cast member not playing **MADE***].

> *(That cast member speaks from wherever they are onstage.)*

CAST MEMBER 2. No, that's me.

MISS. Okay, then you're definitely *[name of cast member portraying **MAN***].

MAN. No, that's me.

MISS. Well, hell's bells! How can I be expected to keep you all straight?

> *(**MADE** slaps **MISS**.)*

This parody is an insult to my –

> *(**MADE** slaps **MISS** again.)*

How am I supposed to –

> *(**MADE** slaps **MISS** again.)*

Understand my role in this –

> *(**MADE** slaps **MISS** again.)*

> *(This time, **MISS** feels the slap. She holds her cheek in disbelief, falling to the ground.)*

> *(Then she rises dramatically, making a long trek across the space. She stumbles. Everyone watches. She catches her balance, continuing on. Eventually she turns to face everyone. The actor performs the following naturalistically – no heightening, lets go of **MISS** completely.)*

I'd like to apologize on behalf of my entire race.

That's what you want, isn't it?

I am so fucking sorry that I was born white and that there is racism in the world and that you have to suffer through it, but what do you want me to do, huh? Huh? Give up my own life? Wade around miserably, feeling bad about a bunch of shit that happened before I was even born? Anyone? Does anyone have an actual answer or are we all just supposed to join in this grand pity party?

What do you wanna do? Come into my house? Make it your own? Huh? Huh?

> *(Laughs.)*

O yes, that's what you want, isn't it?

To come into the house my daddy built with his brothers and uncles and grandfathers and grandmothers and sisters and nieces.

You wanna come out of the fields into this house and put your feet up. Well, go ahead if it'll make you feel better.

MAN. *(No "negro dialect.")* Man snaps his fingers *(snap)* so Miss can see what's in the floorboards of what she thinks is her house.

> *(**MISS** looks around, eyes wide.)*

A truth sneaks in.

> *(Now, the actor is **MISS** again.)*

MISS. Miss looks here and there for the comfort of a fellow White.

> *(**MISS** looks here and there melodramatically.)*

Finding none, she stumbles

falls

gets back up

stumbles and falls again.

Then, the light catching her hair, she turns to the people she's always done her best to help and says:

> *(**MISS** turns to **MAN** and **MADE**. She is dying.)*

There's

got to be

a

better way

for you

to protest than –

MADE. Nope.

> *(**MISS** is dead.)*

MAN. She dead for good?

MADE. Nah. I give her about fifteen minutes.

> (**THREE** *enters from the margins, moving through the space, dropping more paper.*)

THREE. I am carrying my mother's things.
    They are not mine – I mean – they are not mine alone.
    They are mine plus hers.
    They are seventy percent mine and thirty percent hers.
    I carry them because her hands too shaky.
    I carry them because her arms too busy.
    I carry them because –
    because them carry I
    busy too arms her because them carry I
    shaky too hands her because them carry I
    hers percent thirty and mine percent seventy are they
    hers plus mine are they
    alone mine not are they – mean I – mine not are they
    things mother's my carrying am I –

> (**SEVEN** *enters. He's still being followed and is terrified.*)

SEVEN. He's coming fast, y'all.
    He's right up on me but
    I don't
    I don't know him
    And I ain't steal nothin
    I swear I ain't
    Wait
    I do
    Maybe I do know him
    He looks kinda familiar –

> (*And* **SEVEN** *is on the run again.* **ONE, EIGHT,** *and* **FOUR** *enter and sprinkle more paper on the ground, preparing.* **FIVE** *and* **SIX** *speak.*)

FIVE. I gotta say, though,

I once knew a dude whose friend could never hear him when he said, "You're eating me."

So he kept on eating himself alongside his friend so the friend wouldn't get embarrassed, you know?

SIX. Yeah? What happened?

FIVE. He ate himself all the way down to just a mouth and a throat.

SIX. O shit. What'd his friend do?

FIVE. She didn't notice.

SIX. O. That sounds normal.

SEVEN. He's coming faster

He got a look in his eyes like he –

THREE. I am carrying my sister's things.

They are not mine – or rather – they are not mine alone.

They are mine plus hers.

Her palms too dry

Her head too full.

I am carrying my brother's things.

They are not mine – or rather – they are not mine alone.

They are mine plus his.

They are seventy percent mine and thirty percent his.

I carry them because his chest too mouth too slack too riddled too big too brawny too tight

too much to handle to do

too bad too bad too bad

too bad too bad too bad

This is my face.

This is the face that I have.

It is a pretty good face, don't you think?

No. Don't answer that.

This is my face.

The one I was given when faces were being given out.

The job of a face is to tell the outside what the inside is thinking.

Or to hide what the inside is thinking from the outside.

Is that not the job of a face?

And if it is, is my face doing its job?

EIGHT & FOUR. Don't answer that.

This is my face.

My mother pulled it from her ribs

ironed it, shined it and here it is.

A bit too much starch but Mom did what she had to do.

FIVE & SIX. This is my face. It is kind of soggy because my father thinks it is a handkerchief. He cried into it when his mother died. I can't get it dry. I can't get it dry.

SEVEN. He's

y'all

He won't stop

Y'all he won't –

TWO. BANG

> (**SEVEN** *falls, dead. A moment of horrified stillness as they look at* **SEVEN**, *whose fall is cushioned by what should be lots of shredded white paper.*)

MADE. Made doesn't have any kids.

Made doesn't have any kids and it is after the boy's been filled with holes

the body washed and sobbed over

and hymned over and placed into the ground.

It is when the news cycle has cycled and

his name has gone cold on nearly everyone's tongue.

It is evening time and Made stands grinding glass

and wishing.

She wishes she'd had The Talk with her Son.

She wishes she'd sat him down

placed a firm hand on his shoulder and said:

Son,

When a white boy says, "Don't worry, you'll be clean like me some day."

Find the nearest pile of dog shit

and rub his miserable face in it.

When a white woman crosses the street because she sees you coming

Laugh maniacally. Give that bitch somethin to run away from.

When white folks call the police on you for just standing there

for merely being in time and space

reach into their chests, pull their hearts out

and eat them.

Made wishes, Made wishes.

When you've had a seizure on a train and an old white man in a suit

drags you onto the platform so he won't be delayed getting home

Wake your ass up

put your hands around his throat

and put that motherfucker on the tracks. See if that get him home faster.

When you're minding your own business and some monster stabs you in the neck

Go ahead and die, Baby. Die easy.

But then I want you to come back in thirty days

and when you find him

skin him alive

strip by strip of skin.

Take your time

I wantcha to do it strategically.

Do his eyelids first

so he get to watch.

'Cause they ain't learnin. You throwin words but it ain't working.

You marchin, you screaming through a bullhorn but you dead and they smilin and I can't have it. I can't have it no more.

Made wishes O Made wishes.
and she grinds that glass and she burns and she burns
and she burns
O god
She burns.

> (**MADE** *sees the others around her.*)

but

there's a whole lotta ghosts up in here
spirits in the margins lookin at Made
lookin at me like they think
I should turn back.
Give you less things to destroy.
It's nothing personal, I swear.
I'm just a bit tired of your face lookin like it be lookin.
It's everywhere.
On my coffee mug. Over my shoulder. In my cereal. In
my shoes.
On my chest.
Headlining my newspaper.
Everywhere, everywhere.

> (*As the following speaking occurs, all
> continuously circle* **SEVEN**'s *body, building
> the intensity of their movement and voices as
> it progresses.*)

ONE & TWO. Comin outta my iPod sounding but not
looking like me. On every screen. On every screen. On
every screen. In the thread count of my sheets. At the
beginning of this sentence.

ONE, TWO, THREE & FOUR. Where the sidewalk ends. On the
moon. On my soft palate. Down the street. Up the block.
In my secrets. All up in the tofu. In Egypt. Overhead in
a chopper. At the front of the submarine. In both the
blockbuster and the flop. On the board. Treading the
boards. In the dictionary. In the thesaurus.

ONE, TWO, THREE, FOUR, FIVE & SIX. In the essay. In the footnote. In my uterus. Folded into my wallet. On the time stamp. In the credits. On the dotted line. Under my dick. On the bumper of my car. In the crease of my inner arm. In the promise. At the start and finish lines.

ONE, TWO, THREE, FOUR, FIVE, SIX & EIGHT. On the beach. On the brochure. In my spit. In the ozone. On the dirt road. In my dreams (both day and regular). Past the stop sign. Behind the war zone. In the map key. Next-door to the salon. In the mayoral race. On the court. In the court. Where my lips are split. Picking up the crumbs. In satellite. In stereo. En route. In season (always). In the season consistently. In the musculature. In the tremor and the sucked teeth. In Mama's Blues. In Daddy's screams. In the mirror and so I must close the door on you.

> *(All give a group yell. Expulsion, expansion, cleansing of the spirit and the space. This takes as long as it needs to.* **FOUR** *waits for it to die out before she speaks. By now everyone is in a tight circle around* **SEVEN***'s body.)*

FOUR. The people speak the names.

> *(***FOUR** *goes to each participant in the circle individually with a bowl filled with small pieces of red ribbon. Each* **PARTICIPANT***, save for* **SEVEN***, recites the following:)*

PARTICIPANT. "My name is *[name of participant]*. I send something up in the name of *[name of someone lost to anti-Black violence]* who was born on *[birthdate of lost one]* and taken away on *[date lost one was murdered]*."

> *(The* **PARTICIPANT** *then takes two handfuls of shredded paper.)*

FOUR. Black people.

ALL. Yeah.

FOUR. Black people.

ALL. Yeah.

FOUR. Speak the names.

> *(All speak the name of the lost one they're honoring in unison.)*

Speak the names.

> *(All speak the name of the lost one they're honoring in unison.)*

May they what?

ALL. Rest in power.

FOUR. May they what?

ALL. Rest in power.

FOUR. Black people.

ALL. Yeah.

FOUR. Drop something.
Black people.

ALL. Yeah.

FOUR. Drop something.

> *(All slowly and silently let the ribbon fall from their hands and onto **SEVEN**'s body. An offering. When all of the ribbon has been dropped:)*

Black people.

ALL. Yeah.

FOUR. They will call this a riot.

ALL. Yeah.

FOUR. The will call this a riot.

ALL. Yeah.

FOUR. What a riot.

ALL. *(Spoken. Sarcasm.)* Ha ha ha.

FOUR. What a riot.

ALL. Ha ha ha.

FOUR. Black people.

ALL. Yeah.

FOUR. Get quiet.

The people are quiet for a full minute to honor the dead.

> *(All is still for a full minute. Respect this full minute. They help* **SEVEN** *to stand and join the circle.)*

You mad?

ONE. Ah!

FOUR. You mad?

TWO. Ah!

FOUR. You mad?

THREE. Ah!

FOUR. You mad?

FIVE. Ah!

FOUR. You mad?

SIX. Ah!

FOUR. You mad?

EIGHT. Ah!

FOUR. You mad?

SEVEN. Ah!

FOUR. Black people.

ALL. Yeah!

FOUR. Black people.

ALL. Yeah.

FOUR. You mad?

ALL. Ah!

FOUR. You mad?

ALL. Ah!

FOUR. You mad?

> *(The following song/chant is confrontational. They address the viewers and maybe move into the audience.)*

ALL.

WHO ME?

I'M NOT MAD AT ALL
I'M DRESSED TO THE NINES
AND I'M GOIN TO A BALL

WHAT'S THAT?
THAT'S WHERE MY PEOPLE STAY
WE INSIDE, WE OUTSIDE, WE THERE
WE ON THE WAY

TO WHAT?
TO WHAT IT'S GONNA BE
THE MESS AND THE MESSAGE
THE PEOPLE IN THE STREETS

WE FALLIN WE STANDING
WE DANCIN IN THE LIGHT
WE KICKIN, WE RUNNIN
WE PLAYIN AND WE FIGHT LIKE

DOO DOO DOO DOO
DOO DOO DOO DOO

AH AH AH AH
AH AH AH AH

> *(All return to the playing space and stand in a circle.)*

FOUR. Black people.

ALL. Yeah.

FOUR. Send it up!
Send it up!
Send it up!

> *(They send it up. This is a rigorous movement to rid the body/spirit of things that need ridding. Like shaking off a haint. Like a self-exorcism. The participants should take all the time this needs. When this dies down, **EIGHT** sings a solo.)*

EIGHT.

ONE DAY I'M GON PUT ON MY BEST SHOES
ONE DAY I'M GON PUT ON MY BEST SHOES

ONE DAY I'M GON PUT ON MY BEST SHOES
AND SET MY FEET TO WALKIN
ONE DAY I'M GON PUT ON MY BEST SHOES

ONE DAY I'M GON CUT OFF ALL MY HAIR
ONE DAY I'M GON CUT OFF ALL MY HAIR
ONE DAY I'M GON CUT OFF ALL MY HAIR
AND NEVER MIND THEM WATCHING
ONE DAY I'M GON CUT OFF ALL MY HAIR

ONE DAY I'M GON SEE YOU STANDING THERE
ONE DAY I'M GON SEE YOU STANDING THERE
ONE DAY WHEN I SEE YOU STANDING THERE
I HOPE YOU KNOW YOU KNOW ME
ONE DAY I'M GON SEE YOU STANDING THERE

ALL.

ONE DAY I'M GON LOOK UP TO THE SKY
ONE DAY I'M GON LOOK UP TO THE SKY
ONE DAY I'M GON LOOK UP TO THE SKY
AND FIND IT WON'T BE FALLING
ONE DAY I'M GON LOOK UP TO THE SKY

HEY Y'ALL.
HEY
HEY Y'ALL.
HEY
HEY Y'ALL HEY Y'ALL HEY Y'ALL.
HEY

> *(During the course of the "Hey Y'all" portion of the song, each person takes turns taking space and dancing in the center of the circle. This is joyful. Once everyone has had their turn, they return to seriousness.* **TWO** *addresses us.)*

TWO. Earlier, many of you wrote some things down you'd like to offer to Black people.

I'd like to share a few of them now for anyone present and send them up to those no longer with us. Please sit forward in your chair and plant your feet as we do this.

(Someone hands **TWO** *a few of the notes written in the beginning of the ritual. It's probably best to screen these.)*

TWO. I'll read what's written and we'll all repeat it, sending it up. Here we go.

(He reads three notes and asks the audience to repeat them three times each.)

We've all seen, heard and experienced a lot this evening.

As we think about these things, let's take a collective breath. Please join us if you need to. On three. One, two, three.

(Breath.)

Again.

(Breath.)

And one last time.

(Breath.)

The ritual is not over.

In a minute we'll disperse for the final portion.

But, these are our last few moments together as one group

so we want to thank you

(They gather for bows as he speaks.)

we want to thank you

we want to thank you for being here with us.

(Bows.)

At this time, we'd like to invite the Black folks who are present to stay in this space and we invite our non-Black friends to head out into the lobby where someone is waiting to greet you. We'll take just a very few minutes to do this and we'll continue.

(To the Black Folks, in their space.)

Let's form a circle.

If there is anyone here who would like to speak the name of someone we've lost to anti-Black violence, please take a step forward.

(People may step forward to speak a name. Allow as much or as little time for this as necessary.)

Let's form a circle together.

We're gonna take a moment just to be with each other.

Look at the face of each person in this circle.

(This happens.)

The idea that we're separate is an illusion.

Racism will make you feel lonely but no one here is alone.

We've got a strong tradition of community.

We've got each other.

And

We've got the ghosts, the ancestors in the margins rooting for us.

Now I'm gonna give some calls and I'd love for y'all to respond with "yeah."

Black people

Yeah

Black people

Yeah

Black people

Yeah

You beautiful people

Yeah

You creative people

Yeah

You strong people

Yeah

You tender people

Yeah

You smart people
Yeah
You funny people
Yeah
You varied people
Yeah
You fly people
Yeah
You sky people
Yeah
You dark-skinned people
Yeah
You light-skinned people
Yeah
You middle-of-the-road-brown people
Yeah
You passing people
Yeah
You queer people
Yeah
You Black Panther people
Yeah
You blues people
Yeah
You quiet people
Yeah
You book-read people
Yeah
You hood people
Yeah
You field holler people
Yeah
You trans people
Yeah

You ancient people
Yeah
There is love, Black People.
Yeah
There is love, Black People.
Yeah
Right here, Black People.
Yeah
Do you feel it, Black People?
Yeah
Do you feel it, Black People?
Yeah
You're here, Black People.
Yeah
You're here, Black People.
Yeah
And you belong, Black People.
Yeah

Thank you all so much for being with us.
We hope this has been useful to you.
We invite you to head out into the lobby where we hope
you'll keep the conversation going.

> *(Meanwhile, a **FACILITATOR** reads the following
> to the Non-Black Folks in their space once
> they have made their way outside.)*

FACILITATOR. The following is a note from the creator of
What to Send Up When it Goes Down.
A good friend once told me that we each have a
different job where challenging racism is concerned.
She spoke to the ways she could use her privilege as
a white woman to dismantle the white supremacist
ideology that contributes to the deaths of so many
people. As a Black woman and writer, I am uniquely
positioned to create a piece of theatre focused on
making space for Black people. This is one way I can

contribute. This is my offering. I'd like to end this ritual by challenging you to consider what *you* are uniquely positioned to offer. As a non-Black person, what is a tangible way you can disrupt the idea responsible for all of these lives needlessly taken?

My hope is that you will consider this deeply.

My further hope is that your consideration will turn to action.

End of Play

Sun Come Up

Music and Lyrics: Aleshea Harris

Swung

Sun come

up___ Shine on me. Can't

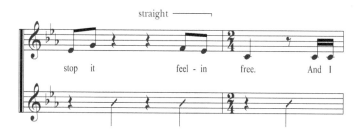

stop it feel - in free. And I

got that love_____ From be-low and a-bove___

One Day

Music and Lyrics:
Aleshea Harris

One day I'm gon put on my __ best shoes.

One day I'm gon put on my best shoes.

One day I'm gon' put on my __ best shoes and set my feet to walk-in

One day I'm gon' put on my best shoes.

One day I'm gon' cut off all __ my hair

One day I'm gon-na cut off all __ my hair

One day I'm gon cut off all __ my

hair and nev - er mind them watch - ing

One day I'm gon cut off all __ my hair.

One Day - p.3

One day I'm gon see you stand - ing there ___

One day I'm gon see you stand - ing there

One day when I see you stand - ing

there I hope you know you know me

One day I'm gon see you stand - ing there.

One day I'm gon' look up to ___ the sky ___

One day I'm gon look up to ___ the sky

One day I'm gon' look up to ___ the sky and find it won't be fal - ling

One day I'm gon look up to__ the sky.

Hey y'all hey   Hey y'all hey   Hey y'all hey y'all hey y'all hey

Heyy'all hey   Heyy'all hey   Hey y'all hey y'all hey y'all hey

Rosebush

Music and Lyrics:
Aleshea Harris

Don't   see   noth - in'   but   me.

Me   on   the   side - walk   me   on   the   fence.

Am   I   go - ing   cra - zy   it   don't   make   no   sense.

Sear - chin'   for   that   gar – den   un – der   ground   Went

hunt - in' for that hid - den trea - sure al - most drowned.

♩=98, Slower - Swung 8ths

Ma - ma where'd you hide that rose bush

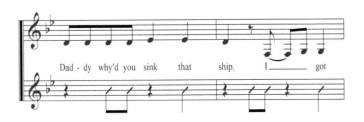

Dad - dy why'd you sink that ship. I got

noth - in' to put in my jew - lry box And I'm

Tempo I

rit.

CPSIA information can be obtained
at www.ICGtesting.com
Printed in the USA
LVHW020333050222
710170LV00013B/2068

9 780573 707919